MW00743868

A Small Collection of Christian Prayers

By Tom Copple

With Introduction by Dr. David Veum

May this book be a blessing to you and yours

— Tom Copple

ISBN 978-1-300-18967-1

Special thank you to –

My Parents, My Grandma, and Dr. Veum for your support and encouragement to me in this project.

And also thank you Bethel Lutheran Brethren Church for letting the front of their sanctuary be used for making the cover of this book.

Indeed, I know the plans I have thought of for you, declares the Lord, plans of peace and not harm, to give you a future and hope.

Jeremiah 29:11

A note to the reader,

Some of these prayers are related to Scripture passages, the Nicene Creed, and the sacraments, and I have made note of them on the respective prayers in italics.

Introduction

Many have sought to define prayer:

"A two-way conversation with God."

"The breath of the soul."

"Letting Jesus into our need."

The prayers in this collection imply this definition:

"The confession of our need and of our faith."

I have known their author since he was a freshman in college. Tom had recently arrived at an evangelical faith after a journey from Catholicism, to neo-paganism, to simple faith in Christ for the forgiveness of sins. His journey has led him to a deep appreciation for Scripture, for the Christian confessions, and for the church of Jesus Christ.

This collection offers the one who prays brief, concrete language in poetic style to confess both spiritual need and faith in our Lord. I commend these prayers to you for your life in Christ.

David Veum

September 12, 2012

Lord Jesus Christ,

Head over your body, the church

Our Lord, we humbly ask that you

Sustain your body and our home, the church,

With the faithful proclamation of your word

And administration of your sacraments.

Please let your church be found faithful in this mission it has

been given.

In your name we pray,

Amen.

Holy Spirit, Lord, Giver of Life

In the creed, it says you spoke by the prophets.

Please Holy Spirit, we ask that in this time,

That you come and speak through the preachers in the church

As you did through the prophets of old.

We ask this Lord for as your word says,

Your word gives life that we so desperately need,

In Jesus' name, we humbly pray.

Amen.

Nicene Creed

Our Father,

Who art in heaven.

Holy is your name.

The earth is yours, and all that is in it.

You reign over it,

And nothing happens that doesn't further your will.

Father, we humbly ask that your will be done on earth as it is in

Heaven.

Amen.

The Lord's Prayer

O Lord Jesus, blessed are those who walk in your ways.

This is impossible for me to do on my own, but with your grace,

Anything is possible.

Lord Jesus Christ, thank you for sustaining and keeping me.

In your holy name I pray.

Amen.

Psalm 1

Jesus Christ, our good shepherd,

Lead me in the path that you have chosen for me.

Please Jesus, you know the way

That you have desired for me.

But I am weak, I am easily distracted, I am unable to follow you

Unless you bring me, as the good shepherd does.

Thank you, Jesus Christ,

Amen.

Thank you Lord Jesus Christ,

Conqueror of death, the one who reconciles

Us to the Father.

On the day we meet face to face, we will feast in triumph

Because of what you have done for us, Jesus.

Please Lord Jesus, may we hasten that day when we get to

Be with you, and may we testify down here to that anticipation.

This we pray. Amen.

Isaiah 25:6-9

Lord Jesus Christ, our saving King

You are the authority, you're our ruler.

According to the apostle Paul, we are your ambassadors,

Please aid your faithful in representing you,

Our love and respect for you are imperfect,

But by your grace, they grow.

Thank you Lord Jesus Christ,

Amen.

Jesus Christ, Son of God.

You, who were there in the beginning, thank you.

Thank you for coming down to us from heaven,

And being lifted up on the cross,

To bring us to the Father. Thank you.

This we pray, Amen.

Dear Jesus Christ,

By the act of baptism,

We are buried with you in death,

And risen with you in your resurrection.

Dear Jesus, please let us live in the light of being buried

And risen with you.

For we are forgetful and need to be reminded of this dear truth.

We thank you, Lord Jesus Christ.

Amen.

Baptismal vows

Lord Jesus Christ, Son of God, Savior of Man.

Lord, in your supper, you have given me

Your precious body in the bread,

And your blood in the drink.

You have done this that I may live in communion

With you and that I may have life.

To you Lord Jesus, I am eternally grateful.

Amen.

Holy Communion

Praise be to you Lord Jesus Christ,

In the Scriptures, we see that obedience brings blessing

But we know that we are not obedient.

We are fallen and disobedient children,

And we don't deserve the Father's blessing

Yet we are blessed by Him solely by your work Jesus

Thank you Lord Jesus Christ.

In your name we pray,

Amen.

Leviticus 27

Merciful God, gracious savior,

You have restored the joy of your salvation to those you have

Called out. For this reason, O Lord, let us not cease in giving

You praise.

This we humbly pray, in Jesus' name,

Amen.

Psalm 51

Lord Jesus Christ, savior of man,

Thank you for being my light, and pleading my case.

I have sinned and fallen in darkness,

But you have raised me to light by your grace.

Amen.

Micah 7:8-9

Glory be to you, Lord Jesus Christ,

Our Creator and Redeemer,

For by you all things are made, and we draw life;

And by you, we are reconciled to the Father.

Please Jesus, may we testify to your goodness and our hope in You.

We pray this Jesus, to you.

Amen.

Colossians 1

May the Lord Jesus Christ raise you in his grace,

Lead you by his hand,

And may he call you by your name.

Glory and honor to the Son of God,

Our Savior, Jesus Christ, Now and Forever.

Amen.

Blessing

Lord Jesus Christ,

I stand hollow before you.

Please pour out Your spirit and grace to me,

That I can be faithful to You and a blessing

To others in Your name.

Please make sure I remember that

I am not alone.

In Your name, I pray,

Amen.

O, that I may praise

The Lord with all my soul.

That I may praise Him with all

My being,

Amen

Lord Jesus Christ,

Here I stand, broke open and putting

Myself before you.

I have nothing to earn your favor and I have

Done much to earn your wrath.

I confess to you Jesus Christ,

That my sins of omission and commission

Have nailed you to the cross.

I lay them bare before you and I am sincerely

Sorry for committing them.

For your mercy precious Jesus, I am eternally grateful.

Amen.

Confession

Heavenly Father,

Your word testifies to us who your son is,

And is a lamp to our feet, which lightens our way.

May the Holy Spirit enlighten us by your word, and

May we live by it, on the paths that you have laid

Before us.

We pray this Lord, in Jesus' name.

Amen.

Psalm 119:105

Holy Lord,

Through the work of your Son,

We became your chosen people,

Your holy nation.

Help us to be the shining city on

The hill you have called us to be,

And draw people to you, and to your son.

This we most humbly pray in Jesus' name,

Amen

1 Peter 2:9

Merciful Jesus, our saving king,

You have conquered the evil one

At the cross.

Yet he seeks to deprive us joy in

The victory that you have already won.

Please remind us Jesus, that you will

Preserve us, and do justice for us

At your appointed time.

This we humbly pray Lord Jesus Christ,

Amen.

Lord God, our Creator and Redeemer,

You know the paths and destinations

You have planned for us.

Please strengthen our faith O Lord,

For we do not see what you see,

But we have your promise,

That you work all things for the good of those

Who love you.

Please strengthen our faith Lord, and

Grow our confidence in you, and your promise.

We pray this Lord, in Jesus' Name,

Amen.

Come Holy Spirit, our Comforter and our Advocate.

Jesus Christ, our Savior has sent you to us so that

We won't be alone.

As the darkness may rise and doubts may come,

Pull us that much closer to you.

Remind us that we are not alone,

And give us strength to face the day,

Whatever may come.

We pray this in Jesus' name,

Amen.

John 14:25

Dear Jesus,

As this day begins,

I humbly ask that you lead me today,

That my relationships point to you Jesus,

And that what I do shows people my love

For you.

This I pray Lord Jesus,

Amen.

Morning Prayer

Lord Jesus Christ, merciful savior.

As my day ends, I thank you.

Thank you for guiding me through it.

You have graciously led me,

And mercifully raised me.

Thank you Jesus, my savior.

Amen

Evening Prayer

Glorious Jesus, our risen King.

You conquered death and gave us life.

Let us not cease to give you praise

Please let us hold your banner high

And praise your name.

This we pray Lord Jesus,

Amen.

Lord Jesus, Son of God,

The one who brings us to the Father.

Please, may we behold you as the

Lamb of God who takes away the sins

Of the world.

Because of our sins, we stand

Separated from the Father,

But you take away our sins Jesus,

And reconcile us to Him.

Lord Jesus Christ, the Holy Lamb of God,

Thank you for what you have done for us.

Amen.

Lord Jesus Christ, God Incarnate,

Please grow our passion for your Scriptures,

For Your Holy Scripture testifies to who you are,

And may we look to what your word says.

Amen.

Dear Jesus, our precious savior,

Your bride, the church, has been given a magnificent mission,

The spreading of Your gospel.

Please let Your bride, the Church, and us, her members,

Not be found lacking in this mission.

In Your word, we see that people will not be saved apart

From this gospel,

Please, by Your grace, may we spread Your gospel.

May the gates and strongholds of Hell fall at the sound of

Your name.

In Your name we pray Lord Jesus,

Amen.

Holy Lord,

Our sustainer and solid rock, in our time of need,

When the clouds cast us in darkness,

And when the trials of this life lay siege on us,

Let us O Lord, rest comfortably in your providence.

For you will not let the evil one seize us,

From your hand.

And at your appointed time you will

Vindicate our faith in you.

Thank you for being our strength and our rest O Lord,

In Jesus name,

Amen.

Lord Jesus Christ,

Clothe us in You and Your righteousness.

Because we have been baptized into You Jesus,

We are no longer

Jew or Gentile,

Slave or Free,

Male or Female,

But in You we are one and made heirs

To the promise of Abraham,

Which is You.

Thank you Lord Jesus Christ,

Amen.

Galatians 3:26-29